Charlie's MONSTER

A HALLOWEEN TALE

Written by T. Appleton

Illustrated by Ross Kirk

Join Charlie and Bobby online! @CharlieandBobby

 @TheTalesOfCharlieAndBobby

Charlie the fish has a sweet life. He is a handsome and happy fish with beautiful bright colors.

Charlie lived at the local pet store and one day a little boy named Bobby came in and adopted Charlie.

Charlie was so happy to be going home with his new friend Bobby!

Charlie now lives in an abandoned shipwreck in a roomy fish tank and enjoys all the fish food he wants.

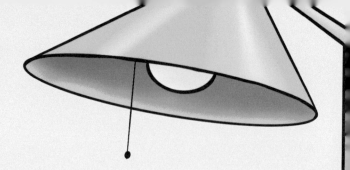

But lately, there have been some strange things happening around Charlie's new home.

First, he begins to see ghosts and skeletons appear all over the house.

Then, out of nowhere Bobby's mother replaces Charlie's shipwreck with a scary ghost house!

Next, someone placed a witch's pot filled with candy by the front door.

Charlie stares at the pot full of candy in awe.

Then all the sudden, Bobby bursts through the front door and races straight upstairs. And for the very first time he didn't even greet Charlie.

Suddenly a light comes on from upstairs and Charlie gets excited.

But then, he hears something strange from...up there!

"Eeh! Oooh!"

He swims to the back of his ghost house and peeks out from behind. He is terrified at what he sees!

It's a MONSTER!
And it's coming down
the stairs making a
terrible noise!

"Grrr..."
Oooh!"

Charlie swims into his house,
a place he would never dare
enter until now.

The monster continues to head in Charlie's direction. The monster gets closer...and closer! Charlie is more afraid then ever, even his fins are trembling!

Charlie wonders if the monster has done something to his best friend, Bobby. The thought was more than Charlie could bear. Charlie is filled with terror but knows he must be brave to save his friend. He loves Bobby and if this monster has done something to him he will make him pay!

Charlie knows he only has one option. To get a better look he must turn on the lamp above his fish tank.

Leaving the safety of his ghost house, he swims around and around gathering enough speed to leap out of the tank.

He quickly pulls the cord on the lamp...

...and plops back into the water with a big splash!

Before he takes a breath, he is face to face with the big monster! Charlie cannot believe who is staring him in the face!

It's Bobby!

Charlie is so happy to see his best friend is safe.

"Hello, Charlie! Do you like my costume? Today is Halloween! I love Halloween!"

Charlie looks confused and asks, "What is Halloween?"

"Halloween is when everyone dresses up in costumes and gets lots of candy. I got you a costume too!"
Bobby pulls out a tiny shark mask and fin and puts them on Charlie's back.

Charlie's new costume makes him feel fearless!

Charlie you will get to see all the trick or treaters.
Now remember, the costumes are a lot of fun, but some can be scary, so be brave and enjoy your very first Halloween!

Charlie's
Halloween Safety Tips

🎃 Trick or treat is safer when you walk in groups, with your parents, or a trusted adult. Never trick-or-treat alone.

🎃 When trick-or-treating at night, use a flashlight to help you see and others see you.

🎃 Do not run from house to house always WALK.

🎃 Never enter a home without your parent or trusted adult. Trick-or-treat at well-lit homes, both inside and outside.

🎃 Never accept rides from strangers.

🎃 Before eating your treats, let an adult inspect all your treats for tampering or choking hazards.

🎃 Never eat homemade treats made by strangers. We recommend only eating treats in original factory wrapping.

🎃 If anyone tries to grab you - LOUDLY yell, "This person is not my mother/ father!" Or " This person is trying to take me!"

Made in the USA
Columbia, SC
18 November 2024

46564370R00018